From Death to Life

A True Story of Healing, Hope, and Legacy

By Mike Sandoval

I0616106

For inquiries, speaking engagements, or resources, visit:
www.mikesandoval.org

Dedication

To my mother,
 who chose life and found new life.

To my wife,
 whose faith, love, and partnership make this calling sustainable and beautiful.

And to my son,
 my why — may your life be marked by purpose, passion, and the presence of God.

Table of Contents

Introduction

Your Story Isn't Over

Maybe you picked up this book because you've faced something heavy.
A diagnosis. A loss. A dark season.
Maybe you're in the middle of it right now — trying to hold it together while life feels like it's falling apart.

Or maybe, like my mother once was, you're just tired. Tired of the silence. Tired of the cycles. Tired of wondering if there's any real hope left.

I get it.

This isn't just a story about a 10-year-old boy who survived a brain tumor.
It's about the miracle behind the medicine.
It's about the mother who found faith at rock bottom.
It's about the God who still redeems broken lives.
And ultimately, it's about you — and the hope that your story isn't over either.

There was a time when I didn't think I'd live to see another day.
But what I didn't know then was that God was writing something deeper, something purposeful, even in my pain.
What was meant to destroy me ended up awakening something in my entire family — a faith we didn't know we needed and a future we didn't know was possible.

You don't have to be a religious person to read this.
You don't have to have it all figured out.
All I ask is that you come with an open heart — and maybe a little bit of curiosity.

Because if this book does one thing, I pray it does this:

I pray it reminds you that your breath still has meaning.
That God still writes comeback stories.
That what tried to kill you can't cancel your calling.
And that it's never too late to begin again.

My name is Mike Sandoval.
This is the story that changed my life.

But more than that —
This is the story I pray will spark something in yours.

Let's begin.

Chapter 1: Before the Miracle

I didn't grow up with bedtime stories.
I grew up with sirens, shouting, and the constant scent of drugs and spilled beer.

My earliest memories aren't playgrounds and playdates — they're parties gone sideways, arguments that escalated, and relatives passed out on couches. I was raised in Anaheim, California, surrounded by drugs, alcohol, and gang life. Most of my uncles were in gangs. Some were deep in drugs. My grandparents had come from Mexico, hoping for a better life. But somewhere along the way, pain became normal — and survival became our culture.

We didn't talk about dreams.
We talked about getting through the week.

Eventually, my mom moved us to Arkansas when I was in second or third grade. It was different — quieter. The snow was strange but kind of nice. For a while, life didn't feel as chaotic. But that peace didn't last long.

My stepfather, who was undocumented, got into a car accident. Not long after, we packed up and moved to Utah to live with some of his family. It was supposed to be temporary — just a year — but then he got deported to Baja California.

His parents had a house there, so he had somewhere to go.
We didn't.

Then came the news we didn't want to hear:
"We're moving to Baja to be with him."

None of us wanted to go. We were kids — and we knew. We could feel it in our bones. Something about this move felt wrong.

And we were right.

Life in Baja was hard — not just physically, but emotionally. The community we moved to wasn't even developed. We didn't have a restroom. We barely had electricity. There was no future in sight. No plan. No stability.

What we did have were fights.
 A lot of them.

My mom and step dad drank constantly. Smoked constantly. Argued constantly. Some nights, things got loud. Violent. I was still just a kid, but I knew enough to get my younger brothers out of the house when things got dangerous.

I wasn't just angry at the lifestyle we were living — I was angry that this is what my brothers had to call home.

On my 9th birthday, there was no party. No celebration.
 My mom and stepdad couldn't afford a cake, so they bought me a donut.

Just one.

I remember looking at it. Holding it.
 And then breaking it in pieces so I could share it with my three little brothers.

A donut. That was my birthday.

And somewhere deep inside me, something cracked. I couldn't explain it then, but I had this overwhelming feeling that there had to be more to life than just... surviving.

That's when the headaches started.

At first, they came and went. But then they got worse —
spinning room, can't-stand-up, can't-open-my-eyes kind of
worse. I couldn't get out of bed. My mom didn't know what to
do, so she started bringing me back and forth from Baja to
Anaheim to see doctors.

They ran CT scans. Nothing showed up.

We went back. Then came again. Same results. No answers. Just
pain.

Eventually, it got too hard — too expensive, too exhausting. So
my mom made the decision to leave me with my grandma for a
while. My grandma — strong, old-school, deeply loving — tried
to enroll me in school. But the school required a physical exam.

That physical was the beginning of a discovery that would
change everything.

The doctor noticed something unusual — my vision in my right
eye was deteriorating. He referred me to an optometrist. The
optometrist examined me carefully, then said something no
one expected:

"There's something behind his eye. It's putting pressure on the
nerve. You need to see an ophthalmologist."

So we went.

The ophthalmologist confirmed it: something was pushing on
my optic nerve, damaging my vision.

He didn't hesitate.
 He sent us to an ENT.

And that ENT?
 He didn't wait either.

He scheduled an MRI with contrast.

And that's when we finally got the diagnosis.

Chapter 2: The Day Everything Changed

You never forget the moment your whole life shifts — the moment time slows down and your world goes quiet.

For me, it was in a hospital room staring at the faces of people who didn't have answers.

The MRI had finally given us the truth — a tumor the size of a grapefruit was growing in my brain. There was no medical explanation. No one could understand how the CT scans had missed it. And no one could explain how I had even made it that far.

The moment they told us, my mom broke down crying. Uncontrollably. Loud. Guttural.

I didn't fully understand what was happening. But I understood enough to know something was wrong — really wrong. And when I saw her like that, I did what little boys sometimes do when they're trying to be men.

I told her not to worry.

"Everything's going to be okay," I said softly.

I wasn't trying to be brave. I just didn't want her to cry anymore.

But the truth was... I believed it. Somehow, deep inside, I *knew* I was going to live.
I didn't know much about God back then. No verses. No theology. But what I *did* have was a strange, quiet confidence — like someone was with me. Like I wasn't alone in this.

The doctors didn't waste any time. The tumor was aggressive and the surgery had to happen immediately. They told us we could leave the hospital to grab a light dinner and then return — they were prepping the operating room for first thing in the morning.

There was no time to delay. No time to process.

My family was in shock. The phone calls started. People sent their love, their prayers, their panic. Some tried to come see me, but it was all moving so fast.

I could see it in everyone's eyes — they were terrified.
 Terrified this might be the last time they saw me.

But they kept telling me:
 "You're a strong boy."
 "You're not even scared."
 "You're so calm."

They didn't know I wasn't trying to be calm.
 I just *knew* I wasn't going to die. That's all I could hold onto.

That night, I tried to sleep. I don't remember much. But I remember the morning.

Before the sun came up, they were prepping me. The nurses moved fast. The machines beeped nonstop. Wires, tubes, monitors, blood pressure cuffs. I was hooked up to everything you can imagine.

Then they rolled me down the hallway.

That hallway felt eternal — cold lights, white ceilings, people moving around me while I stared up, trying to memorize the world I wasn't sure I'd see again.

We reached the operating room. It was packed.
Doctors. Nurses. At least 7, maybe 10. I remember the flurry of preparation, the whispering behind masks.

One of the doctors tried to comfort me:
"Everything's going to be okay."

But I beat him to it.
"I know," I said. "Everything's going to turn out just fine."

He paused, surprised. Then nodded.

They placed the mask over my face and began counting down.
5... 4... 3... 2... 1...

Darkness.

The surgery began.

Hours passed. They worked to remove the tumor. But something went wrong.

My body started bleeding — fast, uncontrollably. They couldn't stop it.

They had no choice. They closed me back up early.
The tumor wasn't fully removed.

But the real damage had already been done.

I had lost too much blood.
My body couldn't take it.

I slipped into a coma.

And that's where the miracle begins.

Chapter 3: The Man at the Bedside

The ICU is a place where time stands still.

The lights are dim, but never off. The air smells like antiseptic and grief. Machines beep, whir, and pump in rhythms that feel more mechanical than human. There are no smiles in the ICU — only silent prayers and unspoken fears.

And that's where I was. Motionless. Pale. Surrounded by machines.
While I lay in a coma, my family waited.

They came in rotations — some before work, some after, some in between. Everyone was just... waiting. Waiting for something to change. Hoping I'd wake up. Hoping I'd fight. Hoping I'd live.

But I wasn't fighting.
That's what the doctors were concerned about. I was dying, minute by minute. My body had given up too much blood, and I wasn't responding. They told my mother, "He's not fighting for his life. You need to go in and encourage him. He needs to hear your voice."

But she couldn't move.

She couldn't bear to see me like that. Not her son. Not the boy who had already survived so much.

Everything she had buried — all the trauma, the addiction, the abuse, the broken dreams — came crashing into that moment. She was panicking. Guilty. Angry. And completely helpless. There was nothing she could do to fix it, and for a woman who had survived by staying strong, this broke her.

But eventually, she stood up and walked through those ICU doors.

The hallway leading into the unit felt like walking into a war zone.
 Gurneys rolled past. Alarms rang in other rooms. The cries of loved ones echoed in the background. The tension in the air was thick — like death had settled over the whole floor and wasn't going anywhere soon.

When she reached my bed, she saw me.

Pale. Swollen. Wires running across my body. Tubes in my mouth and nose. I looked lifeless. She broke.

She stood beside me and began to speak.

"Fight, mijo," she whispered through tears. "You have to fight."

She wept as she encouraged me again. "Please don't go. You can't leave me. Not like this."

And that's when she noticed him.

A man standing quietly at the edge of my bed. She hadn't seen him come in. He didn't look like a doctor. No badge. No clipboard. No expression. Just presence.

She focused on me. Until he spoke.

"Do you want your son to be saved?" he asked.

She looked up, startled. "What?"

"I've been with your son for some time now," he said.
 "Then believe in Jesus. Trust Him — and watch what He'll do."

Her world stopped. The room felt like it shrank.

The words hit her — not just in her ears, but deep in her soul. This wasn't a hallucination. She wasn't drunk or high. She was fully present, fully sober... and suddenly, fully aware that something divine was happening.

Desperate, she said, "Of course. Anything for him."

So they prayed. Right there. In the middle of wires and weeping, in the middle of brokenness and fluorescent lights — they prayed.

And when she looked up again... he was gone.

No goodbye. No explanation. Just a memory and a question that would never leave her:

Who was that?

She looked around the ICU. No one had seen him leave. No one even seemed to notice he was there.

But she knew.

She couldn't explain it, but she knew something had shifted. Something holy had stepped into the darkest room of her life.

And the very next day... I woke up.

The doctors couldn't believe it. They had warned my family that, even if I survived, my recovery would be long — months, maybe a year. My body was too far gone. But somehow, I opened my eyes. I moved. I could barely speak, but I remember forcing out a few quiet words.

They were stunned.
"This is unbelievable."
"This is a crazy story."

But my mom wasn't shocked.
She knew the moment God answered.
She had watched death back away.

Within three weeks, I was out of the hospital.
A month later, I was back in school.
The same kid. But not the same story.

>"For nothing will be impossible with God." — Luke 1:37

God didn't just heal me.
He awakened something in my mother.
He used my broken body to begin restoring her broken soul.

She had walked into that ICU with fear, addiction, and pain.
But she walked out with something else:
Hope.

The man disappeared.
But his words never did.

Chapter 4: The Battle After the Miracle

While my body healed, my mother went back to Mexico.

I stayed behind with my grandmother — who recently passed away — and my aunt. They cared for me while I went through the slow, painful process of recovery. Doctors had warned my family that even if I woke up, the road ahead would be long. I would need to relearn how to walk, how to eat, how to speak. Simple things would feel like climbing a mountain.

But the same God who brought me back from the edge carried me through what should have taken months — in just weeks. I left the hospital in three. And within a month, I was back in school.

Physically, I was different.
 There was a massive scar on my head, and staples that looked like something out of a science fiction movie. I started wearing hats to hide it — not because I was ashamed of what God did, but because I was still a kid. And kids can be brutal.

Some days, people would pull off my hat just to laugh.
 Other days, they'd run off with it and make a joke out of my recovery.

It wasn't easy.
 But I kept going.

Meanwhile, across the border, my mom had gone back to her old life. Back to the drinking. Back to the smoke-filled rooms and broken cycles. Back to what she knew. The miracle had stunned her — had shaken something deep — but she didn't know what to do with it. So she buried it.

She tried to move on.
 Tried to return to the survival she was used to.

But something had changed. Even if she didn't want to admit it.

She would sit in silence and reflect. *God really did do a miracle in my son.*
 She couldn't deny it. She had heard the words:
 "Believe in Jesus. Trust Him — and watch what He'll do."
 She had watched it unfold in front of her eyes. She had seen death retreat.

And yet, she wrestled.

She was torn between the lifestyle that numbed her pain and the calling that now tugged on her soul. A part of her was hopeful. But another part was terrified. Surrender felt like a threat to who she had always been.

Then, the unthinkable happened.

My stepfather — the last person anyone would expect to talk about God — looked at her one day and said:

"After everything God did for your son… shouldn't we at least go to church once to give thanks?"

My mom snapped.
 "Don't talk to me about church."

It was instant. Defensive. Angry.

Church was the last thing she wanted to talk about.
 Faith meant change. And change felt like betrayal — of her pride, her wounds, her control.

But my stepfather didn't push. He just waited.

And then, one day, he brought it up again.

"Just once," he said gently. "Just to say thank you."

This time, she didn't yell. But she didn't fold either.
 She wrestled. She reasoned. She tried to shut it down.

Eventually, though, she gave in — with conditions.

"Fine. But only once," she said.
 "And don't tell me about changing who I am."

There was just one problem.
 They didn't have a church to go to.

But my stepfather remembered something.

"Hey, I saw a church the other day on my way home from work.
I hadn't noticed it before. Maybe we could try that one."

It wasn't a plan. It wasn't a spiritual strategy.
 It was just... the next step.

So she agreed.
 Not with joy. Not with surrender. But with resignation.

She would go. Just once. Just to give thanks.

Her heart was still guarded. Her spiritual walls were still up.

But a door had cracked open.

> She had said it would be one visit. Just to give
> thanks.
> But God had something else in mind.

Chapter 5: The Night Everything Changed

They walked to that church on a Wednesday night.

There was nothing extraordinary about the building — just brick walls, faded paint, and a flickering porch light that barely lit the entry. But in the air... there was something else. Tension. Hesitation. A pull neither of them could quite explain.

They didn't drive. They walked.
In silence. Through the cool night. One step at a time.

My mom didn't know what she expected to find.
She had already decided — this was a formality. One visit. Just to say thank you. Nothing more. She wasn't going to change. She wasn't going to open herself up to anything. She was just going to keep her word.

As they reached the door, music leaked through the walls. Soft. Faint. Like someone praying in the form of a song.

They stepped inside.

Dim lights. Unfamiliar faces. The scent of worn pews, stale carpet, and something almost sacred in the air — desperation, maybe. The kind that clings to old church walls where people have cried out to God and hoped He was listening.

The sanctuary was simple. No flashy lights. No polished band. Just a handful of people and a preacher already mid-sermon.

They slid quietly into the last row.

My mother sat guarded — arms crossed, eyes scanning, soul closed.
She was skeptical. Not impressed.

She had lived too much, seen too much, felt too much to be easily moved.

But then... the preacher stopped.

He looked up. Looked straight at her.

And then — he began to speak again. But not like before.

He began describing her life.

He spoke of a woman with a son who had a brain tumor... who had seen a miracle... who had run from faith, but couldn't outrun God.

He began calling out wounds, moments, hidden sins — things she had never shared.
 Things only she and my step dad could have known.

She froze.

Everything inside her tightened. Her breath caught. Her thoughts raced.

She tried to look away. Tried to hide.
 But the words wouldn't stop.

Each one struck like lightning.
 Each one pierced through the walls she had spent years building.

Beside her, my stepfather sat stunned.
 He knew her story. But this? This was something else.

She leaned in and whispered, shaken:
 "Who told him my life?"

She doesn't remember how she got to the altar.
One moment she was in the back row. The next, she was on her knees.

Her body trembled.
Her tears fell in heavy drops that soaked her legs.

She wanted to open her eyes — but couldn't.
All she saw was light. Bright. Blinding. Unshakable.

All she felt was something she had never known before — not addiction, not guilt, not shame, not fear.
This was different.

This… was the presence of God.

What felt like five minutes turned into four hours.

When she finally opened her eyes, the church was empty.
Everyone had left. The service was over.
But something inside her had just begun.

She walked out different.

She didn't have the words.
But she knew what she had experienced was real.

She was sober. Clear. Emotional. Hopeful.
And for the first time in her life, she wanted more.

The same God who had brought her son back from the edge of death…
had now called her into life.

She had come to say thank you.
But God came to say:

"Welcome home."

Chapter 6: A New Legacy Begins

After that night, everything began to shift.

My mother began reading the Bible — and she swears the words spoke to her out loud. Scripture came alive. The stories. The truth. The presence. She couldn't quite explain what had happened to her, so much so that when she went back to church the next time, she actually looked around to make sure no one had spiked her drink.

But it was no trick.
No manipulation.
It was real.

Before she realized it, three months had passed — sober, clear, and hungry for more of God. No more drinking. No more parties. No more numbness. Just conviction, joy, and a sense that she was finally becoming the person she was always meant to be.

From that day forward, my mother's life changed completely.
She gave her life fully to Jesus.

She became a new woman. She started attending church every Sunday and Wednesday. She became a leader. She started praying with boldness, leading with humility, and shining with a light none of us had ever seen in her.

And through her obedience, our family started to change too — especially me.

It was my tumor that led to her transformation.
Her transformation that led to my salvation.
And that near-death moment in my childhood became the spark for a future I never expected.

What started as tragedy became testimony.
 What felt like death became the beginning of new life — for my mom, for me, and for everyone God would allow us to reach.

> "What you meant for evil against me, God meant for good—to bring about this present result, the saving of many lives." — Genesis 50:20

But it wasn't a straight line.

While my mom was growing in Christ, I was drifting.

Junior high was rough. I didn't want anything to do with church. While my mom leaned into her healing, I leaned into the streets. I started hanging with the wrong crowds, getting into fights, chasing the kind of belonging I didn't yet know I already had. I wasn't in a gang officially, but I was close. And honestly, I was drawn to it. In a world where nothing felt consistent, those crews felt like family.

But God wasn't done writing our story.

My mom, now fully committed to Jesus, made one of the hardest decisions of her life — she left my stepdad. He refused to change. He kept drinking. Kept using. And too often, he laid hands on her in ways no woman should ever endure.

So she left.

She moved to another city in Mexico with my brothers. And eventually, she made her way back to Anaheim.

We were relieved.
 Not just because she had finally left him — but because she was free.

She found an apartment and started working to provide for my younger brothers. I was still living with my aunt at the time. But when she was finally able to take me in too, I moved in with her.

And the timing... felt divine.

I was right on the edge of throwing my life away — right on the edge of joining a gang and running with the wrong crowd. But now I was living under the same roof as a woman who had been radically changed by Jesus.

She invited me to church constantly.
I declined constantly.

I didn't want to go. I wanted to live *my* life — be out with friends, feel free. I didn't want Jesus. I wanted fun.

But something was happening beneath the surface.

Around this time, a PE teacher noticed something in me.
He introduced me to basketball — and I fell in love. It became an outlet, an escape, a lifeline. It grounded me. But that's a story for another chapter.

By my senior year, I was ready to graduate and turn 18.
I was already planning my "coming of age" moment — freedom, independence, and doing whatever I wanted.

But something... was tugging at my heart.

I kept getting invited to church. And slowly, I began to go — not because I wanted to, but because something in me couldn't ignore it anymore. Sometimes we'd have small groups at our house with a Spanish-speaking minister. I wasn't really into it. I barely paid attention.

But this one time… he looked at me.

He said, "There's something different about you."

Then he handed me a gift — a book by John Maxwell:
Developing the Leader Within You.

That minister didn't know me. But he saw something.
Just like my mom did.

I was a miracle child. Saved for a reason.
And that reason was starting to catch up with me.

On my 18th birthday — the day I had planned to finally go do
life my way — I got baptized.

I gave my life to Jesus.

I can't fully explain it, but I know God led me there. The same
hand that pulled me out of that coma had been pulling me
toward His heart ever since.

From that day forward, I couldn't get enough of serving.
I started playing bass. Running production. Singing in choirs.
Preaching to youth. Serving anywhere I could. I just wanted to
be in God's house — because I knew firsthand what He could
do with a broken life.

So here's the connection:

My tumor led to the miracle.
The miracle led to my mother's transformation.
Her transformation led to my salvation.
And my salvation… became my calling.

And now, I live to help others find that same healing.

The miracle wasn't the end of the story —
It was the beginning of a new legacy.

Chapter 7: Saved to Serve

After I was baptized, something in me ignited.

It wasn't just about salvation. It wasn't just about healing. It was about purpose.
 I didn't know all the details yet. I didn't have a roadmap. But I knew one thing for sure:

I had to serve.

I started showing up. To youth nights. To small groups. To any opportunity to help — whether it was setting up chairs, playing bass, or handing out flyers. Whatever I could do, I did it. And as I served, something deeper began to grow inside me — not just a passion for the church, but a burden for people.

The more I saw others come to Jesus, the more I wept.
 Because I knew what it was like to be rescued.
 I knew what it was like to be broken — and found.

God had redeemed my pain — and now I wanted to see Him do it again and again in others.

I started studying the Bible with hunger.
 I enrolled in Bible classes, seminars, conferences.
 Eventually, I even stepped into Bible college. I didn't want to just believe — I wanted to be built.

But here's something I never shared until now:
 Before God rescued me, I believed I was an accident.

As a teenager, I learned the truth about how I came into the world — a truth marked by pain, choice taken, and circumstances that no one would wish for. My mother didn't plan for me. And in the eyes of many, she would've had every 'right' to walk away from the pregnancy. But she didn't. She chose life. And because of that, I now get to live with purpose and share the goodness of God.

That knowledge — that I was born from trauma — could have destroyed me.
But instead, it became fuel.
Not shame. Not silence. But *a platform* to testify of God's goodness.

God doesn't just redeem pain.
He builds purpose from it.

Early on, people began to affirm the call on my life. They prayed over me. They spoke life over me. They said, *"You're going to be a leader. God has plans for you."*

At times, I didn't believe them.
It felt too big. Too holy for someone like me.

Even now, I still wrestle:
God, am I really called?
Do I have what it takes?

I had a past.
I had scars.
But I also had grace.

And grace qualifies who pain tried to disqualify.

I started mentoring. Leading. Getting noticed in youth ministry. Worship. Leadership.
My first preaching messages were raw — usually centered around restoration and joy. I talked about the God who can rebuild lives. The God who brings hope to chaos. The God who rescued me.

I preached about growth — even when I was still learning how to grow myself.
 But God gave me those words, and I trusted they were for someone else's healing too.

Eventually, I began leading small groups.
 And I fell in love with it.

Not the platform. Not the mic.
 The people.
 The conversations.
 The community.

I loved opening the Word with others and watching it speak to them the way it once came alive for my mother. I loved building people up. I loved watching the light come back into someone's eyes after a season of darkness.

People started gravitating toward me — but it wasn't really me.
 It was the presence of God in me.

And then came a defining moment.

One night, someone I barely knew came up to me. He didn't just encourage me. He spoke prophetically. He said, *"Mike, you are chosen. Chosen to shepherd. Your past was not a mistake. Use it to reach the broken and lead people to Jesus."*

I stood there, humbled and speechless.
 But deep down, I knew.
 I wasn't just saved.
 I was sent.

From that moment forward, everything I did in ministry had weight.

I didn't want to entertain crowds.
I wanted to equip the called.
I wanted to be a voice for the voiceless.
I wanted to be a hand for the hurting.

My mother's transformation had set off a chain reaction.
Her obedience lit a fire in me.
And now, the legacy of what God did in our family was reaching others.

I wasn't just living a miracle.
I was now becoming part of someone else's miracle.

It didn't stop with Sunday services.
Leadership. Discipleship. Pastoring. Teaching. Mentoring.
This became more than something I did — it became who I was.

And still, to this day, I root for everyone to come to Jesus.
When someone gives their life to God, I celebrate like it's my own child coming home.

I cheer loud. I cry hard.
Because I remember what it's like to be the one people prayed for.

> I was once the boy being fought for in a hospital bed.
> Now, I fight for others — because I know what it's like to need a miracle.

Chapter 8: Growing in Grace

After the high of early ministry came the hidden process of maturity.

People saw me as a leader.
But inside... I was still learning. Still healing. Still wrestling with who I was — and who God was calling me to become.

Because here's the truth:
God wasn't just using me — He was forming me.

The growing pains of ministry were real. They were heavy.
I made mistakes. I missed moments. I sometimes led with more zeal than wisdom.

I had to learn that serving wasn't always glamorous.
Ministry is often messy — and God uses that mess to grow you.

The affirmation I received early on was beautiful — but it was also dangerous if I wasn't careful. I had to wrestle with my pride. I had to make sure the compliments didn't become my identity.

I didn't want to kill my joy by comparing my calling to someone else's.
Still, I often felt like an imposter.

God, am I really called?
Do I have what it takes?

But then I'd remember... this wasn't something I sought out.
This calling found me.
And that realization humbled me again and again.

There were moments I felt overlooked. Other times, misunderstood.
And many times, God began dealing with me directly — not in loud ways, but through quiet correction... and frequent failure.

I had mentors who challenged me to stay rooted — to not follow the hype, but to follow Christ.
They taught me lessons I've never forgotten:

Obedience > Opportunity
Integrity > Influence
Anointing flows through brokenness

Some of the hardest moments were when my past would resurface.

I'd look back on the tumor, the trauma, the violence, the abandonment... and I'd ask:

Why me?
Why did I have to suffer like that?

Then, one day in prayer, I felt the Lord whisper something simple but profound:

"Why not you?"

It wasn't a harsh question. It was holy.
It was as if God was saying, *I trusted you with this pain because I knew what I'd birth from it.*

It was a reframing moment — a turning point.

God hadn't just allowed my life to unfold this way by accident.
He had **strategically positioned** my journey to bring about something bigger than I could see.

And His grace?
It never skips the process.
But it **strengthens** you through it.

Somewhere along the way, there was a shift in my ministry.

I stopped just *doing* ministry.
I started becoming a **shepherd**.

I listened more.
Cared deeper.
Prayed with more compassion.
Led with less ego and more empathy.

And none of it was glamorous.
Most of the roles I served in weren't paid.
I wasn't chasing a platform — I was chasing God's heart.

I served where no one else wanted to.
In the background.
In the shadows.
In the places where people just needed someone to show up
and love them.

And I was okay with that.

What kept me grounded was the Word of God.
What sustained me was the Holy Spirit.
What grew me was *consistency*.

I leaned into mentors. I read leadership books. I listened to
podcasts. I studied the lives of spiritual leaders who led not
with titles, but with *testimonies*.

And when I felt like giving up — when the weight felt too heavy
— it was the **presence of God** that kept me.

I had to learn to lead *myself* before I could lead anyone else.
And I had to do the hard things no one saw — the inner work.

The secret place became more important than the public stage.
The private surrender became the root of any public fruit.

Because growth?
It isn't instant.
It's **intentional**.

And in all of it, I've come to realize:

> "God wasn't looking for perfection.
> He was looking for surrender."

Chapter 9: Sent for More

Sometimes I pause to take it all in — not the titles or the roles, but the story.
From a hospital bed in a coma... to walking in my calling.
From trauma and dysfunction... to peace and purpose.

God didn't just save me *from* something.
He saved me *for* something.

And that something has been unfolding ever since.

My healing, testimony, and transformation began to influence others.
Not because I had it all together — but because I had been through the fire and came out with something to say. God gave me the privilege of walking with people in their valleys. I've had the joy of praying over them, baptizing them, encouraging them, and even officiating their weddings.

Every moment felt like holy ground.

At this point in life, I'm married to the love of my life.
We now have a three-year-old son — our miracle boy.

And now, I have the chance to **rewrite the story forward**.

I didn't grow up with a father.
But now, by God's grace, I get to be one — and I'm doing everything I can to be the kind of father I never had. Not a perfect one, but a present one. A father who covers, leads, protects, prays, and builds a legacy of faith and love in our home.

One day, I shared my story with a man deeply rooted in the gang lifestyle — a path I could've easily ended up on myself. He looked at me and said:

> *"Hearing your journey helped me finally believe that God could redeem mine too. I've been in the gang lifestyle my whole life, but this hit different. It was real. And I'm walking forward with a new purpose and faith in Jesus."*

That's when I realized — I wasn't just sharing my testimony.
I was helping others believe in theirs.

And what made it even more meaningful?
That conversation happened **inside a prison**, during a time I was invited to speak and minister to inmates.
A place most would avoid — but exactly where God sent me.
To remind someone: *your story isn't over.*

Today, I serve as a **young adults coach** and **shepherding elder** at my local church.
People come to me for wisdom, ministry advice, vision, or just encouragement.

Not because I have all the answers, but because I've built real relationships — and people feel safe around someone who's been through it and still kept the faith.

I'm no longer just *serving.*
I'm **shepherding**.

God has entrusted me with more: more people, more spiritual weight, more responsibility. And I don't take that lightly.

The heartbeat of my ministry is simple:

- Preach the good news.

- Make disciples.

- Help the broken.

- And above all — love my family deeply.

My wife and son are everything to me.

My "why" is rooted in gratitude.
I'm grateful for the life I've had — not because it was easy, but because God never wasted a single moment. I'm grateful that out of all the brokenness, He gave me a beautiful family, and now we get to serve together with our whole hearts for the Kingdom.

My wife shares the same heart: to love people, inspire them to follow Jesus, and point them to healing.

My past no longer defines me.
Now, it equips me — to lead with empathy and vision.

Fifteen years into my walk with Christ, I've learned a lot about leadership and discipleship. I'm no expert. But I've leaned into new roles — helping create pathways for discipleship, designing church growth strategies, and building platforms for healing and development.

I'm not trying to be impressive.

I just want people to feel seen.
To know they're called.
To discover what God placed inside them.

That's what my life is about now: **multiplying what God did in me.**
Helping others step into purpose.
Creating environments where restoration is possible — and transformation is inevitable.

Because this isn't just about me.
It never was.

My mother's surrender created a ripple that's still expanding.
She changed the direction of our family.
And now, God is using that decision to build **spiritual families, faith communities, and leaders** who will long outlive my name.

> I'm not just a miracle survivor.
> I'm a message bearer.

> This story was never about spotlight.
> It's always been about salvation.

> And if God can use me...
> He can reach anybody.

Chapter 10: From Death to Life

Coma.
 Healing.
 My mother's surrender.
 My salvation.
 My calling.
 And now, a legacy.

That's my story.

But it's not just about me.
 It's proof that **God still writes new ones.**

If you're reading this and your story feels stuck... if your life feels fractured by trauma, addiction, depression, shame, fatherlessness, or just plain hopelessness — I see you.

Not because I've lived a perfect life.
 But because I've lived a broken one — and watched God redeem every piece.

So let me say this with all the love and urgency I can:

> **If you're reading this wondering if your life has meaning, this is your confirmation: it does.**

You may never face a brain tumor.
 But maybe you're facing your own kind of death — silent battles, private pain, things no one else knows.

And I want you to hear me clearly:
 Your story isn't over.

God didn't just save me for my sake —
 He saved me so I could tell *you* that redemption is real.

Healing is possible.
And your life still holds purpose.

Jesus didn't come to make bad people good.
He came to bring **dead things to life.**

Your heart.
Your faith.
Your future.

He's not offering you religion — He's offering you
resurrection.

If you're ready to receive that kind of grace, here's a simple
prayer:

> **Jesus, I'm tired of running. I'm ready for
> healing.
> I believe You can bring life where death has
> ruled. I give You my heart. I give You my story.
> I trust You with it all. From this day forward, I
> want to walk with You. Amen.**

If you prayed that — or even if your heart just whispered "yes"
in a quiet way — I'm celebrating with you.

But don't stop here.

Here are a few next steps to help you keep walking:

- **Find a local church** that teaches the Word and
  welcomes you like family.

- **Reach out to someone** — a friend, a mentor, even me.
  You don't have to do this alone.

- **Start reading the book of John** in the Bible — begin with the life of Jesus.

- **Join a small group** or Bible study where people are growing together.

DM me. Email me. Reach out. Whatever it takes — don't go back to death when life is calling your name.

Because here's what I've learned:

> Your story matters.
> Your pain has a purpose.
> And **God is not done with you.**

You have the opportunity to begin a new legacy — not just for yourself, but for your family, your community, your future.

You may not have survived a coma —
But you've survived something.
And that's enough for God to work with.

> Don't let your past define you. Let it prepare you.

> *From death to life* wasn't just my story.
> **It can be yours too.**

Continue the Journey: 7-Day Devotional

If this book spoke to your heart, I want to invite you deeper.

I've created a **7-day devotional** called *From Death to Life: Walking Through Your Own Resurrection.* It's designed to help you process your past, lean into God's promises, and walk boldly into your future — one day at a time.

Each day includes:

- A short Scripture

- A personal reflection

- A prayer

- A simple action step

Whether you're healing, rebuilding, or just hungry for more, this devotional will walk with you through it all.

☞ **You can download it at mikesandoval.org**

Let's keep walking — from death to life. Together.

Acknowledgments

To my wife, Reyna — thank you for believing in me when I couldn't see the full picture. Your patience, strength, and encouragement carried me through the writing of this book and far beyond it. You've been more than a partner — you've been a steady reflection of God's grace in my life.

To my family, my church community, my mentors, and every person who spoke life over me during the early days of ministry — thank you. Your faith, your words, and your investment are now reaching others through this book.

And to Jesus — my Savior, my Redeemer, my source — this is all for Your glory. Thank You for bringing me from death to life.

About the Author

Mike Sandoval is a husband, father, and minister with a passion for seeing people encounter the transformative power of Jesus. A survivor of a near-death experience at the age of ten, Mike's life was marked by trauma — but redeemed by grace.

Today, he serves as a shepherding elder and young adults coach at his local church, where he mentors emerging leaders, helps others find purpose in their pain, and develops discipleship pathways for lasting spiritual growth. These pathways are now expanding into a broader platform — a resource he's currently building to equip churches in their mission to disciple well in a post-Christian world.

With over 15 years of ministry and leadership experience, Mike speaks with a voice forged in fire and filled with hope. His heart beats for the broken, the overlooked, and the ready — those on the edge of transformation.

He and his wife, Reyna, are also preparing to launch a faith-based podcast in the winter — a space for real stories, spiritual wisdom, and honest conversations about healing, leadership, and legacy.

Mike lives in California with Reyna and their son — a miracle and a legacy in the making.

You can connect with Mike on Instagram @mike.a.sandoval, visit his website mikesandoval.org, or download his 7-day devotional, *From Death to Life: A 7-Day Journey from Trauma to Resurrection*.